How to increase your Mind Power?

Increase your innovation, learning, organization, management ability in short time

Loren Lawrence

How to use this book 3

    Introduction 3

    Example 4

STARTING 6

ADVANCE 38

ADVANCE   MORE 70

How to use this book

Introduction

Mind mapping is an image-based method of visually expressing knowledge, idea, concepts.

Sometimes you have many ideas come up to your mind for one subject as a glance. But you forget it at the next moment.   Because inside of your brain, much information is monotonous and piece by piece.

Practice mind mapping can make it easier and easier to take out information from your brain, connect the relationship between major subject concerned with information in the brain.

Major ideas are connected directly to the major subject, and other ideas branch out from those major ideas.

Essential Characteristics of Mind Mapping:

- It is often created around a major subject in the central blank block.
- Other ideas branch out from this major subject.
- Associated representations of ideas such as images, words, and parts of words are added in the blank block around the central block.
- Ideas of extended are represented as 'twigs' of the relevant subbranch
- The subbranches form a connected nodal structure

Example

The <u>major subject</u> is "Music."
The <u>branch</u> can be "Jazz", "Country Song", "Piano", or "Drum"...etc.
The <u>subbranch</u> of "Piano" can be "Bar", "Key", or "Piano shop"...etc.
And you can extend the subbranch again.

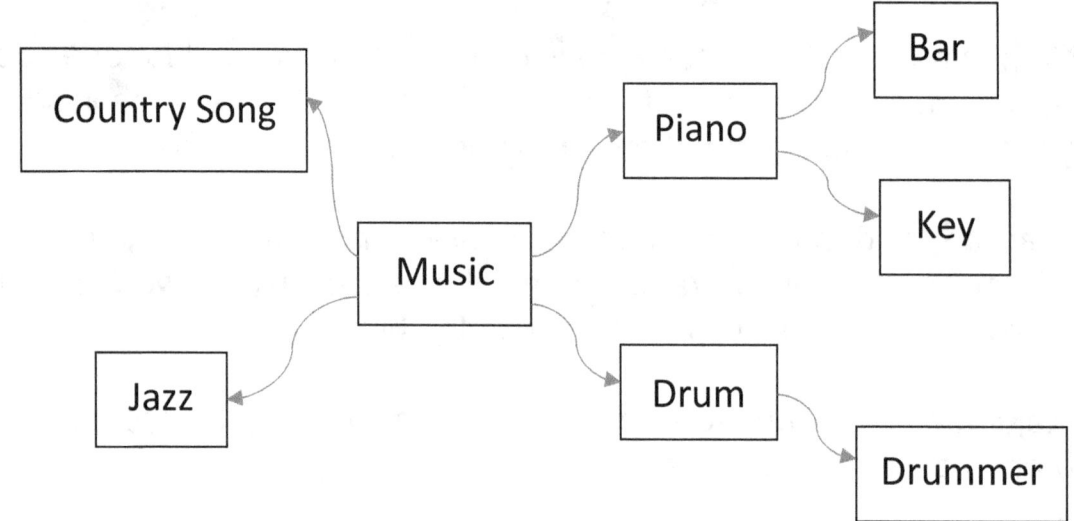

Or, you might connect as follows:

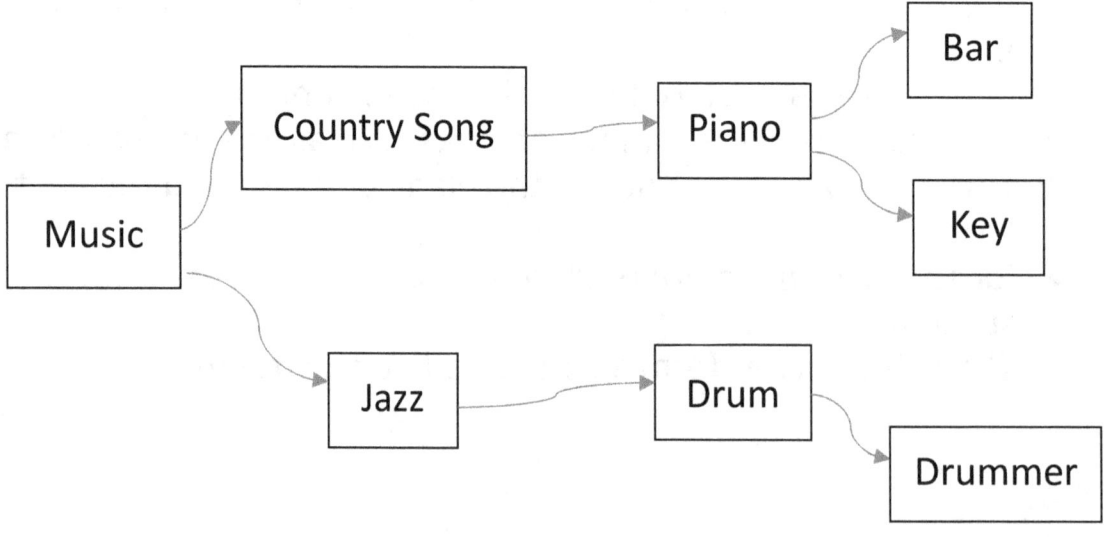

All up to you.

Write down or sketch these ideas what you thought as you set the major subject. You also can find what you like to extend these ideas. It all depends on how far you want to go from the major subject of one mind mapping.

Sketch the connection line between all ideas by yourself.
You can use different colors to write or sketch ideas and connection line as you like. Even you can add the block as you like.

Remember, there is no limit on what is these ideas should be.
And no limitation on how to line these ideas from your mind.

Just let your idea come and record it.

You can develop different mind mapping for a different major subject. Even you can develop different mind mapping at the same major subject again a few weeks later. Maybe it will be different from weeks ago.

Different people might get different mind mapping at the same major subject.

Everyone's mind mapping is unique. You can practice with your family or friend. It's fun.

Practice more, you can find many new ideas you never thought before. Then you can use this skill to innovate, learn, remember, or organizing projects..., etc.

Start to practice your mind mapping now!

STARTING

Major subject

ADVANCE

Major subject

ADVANCE MORE

Major subject

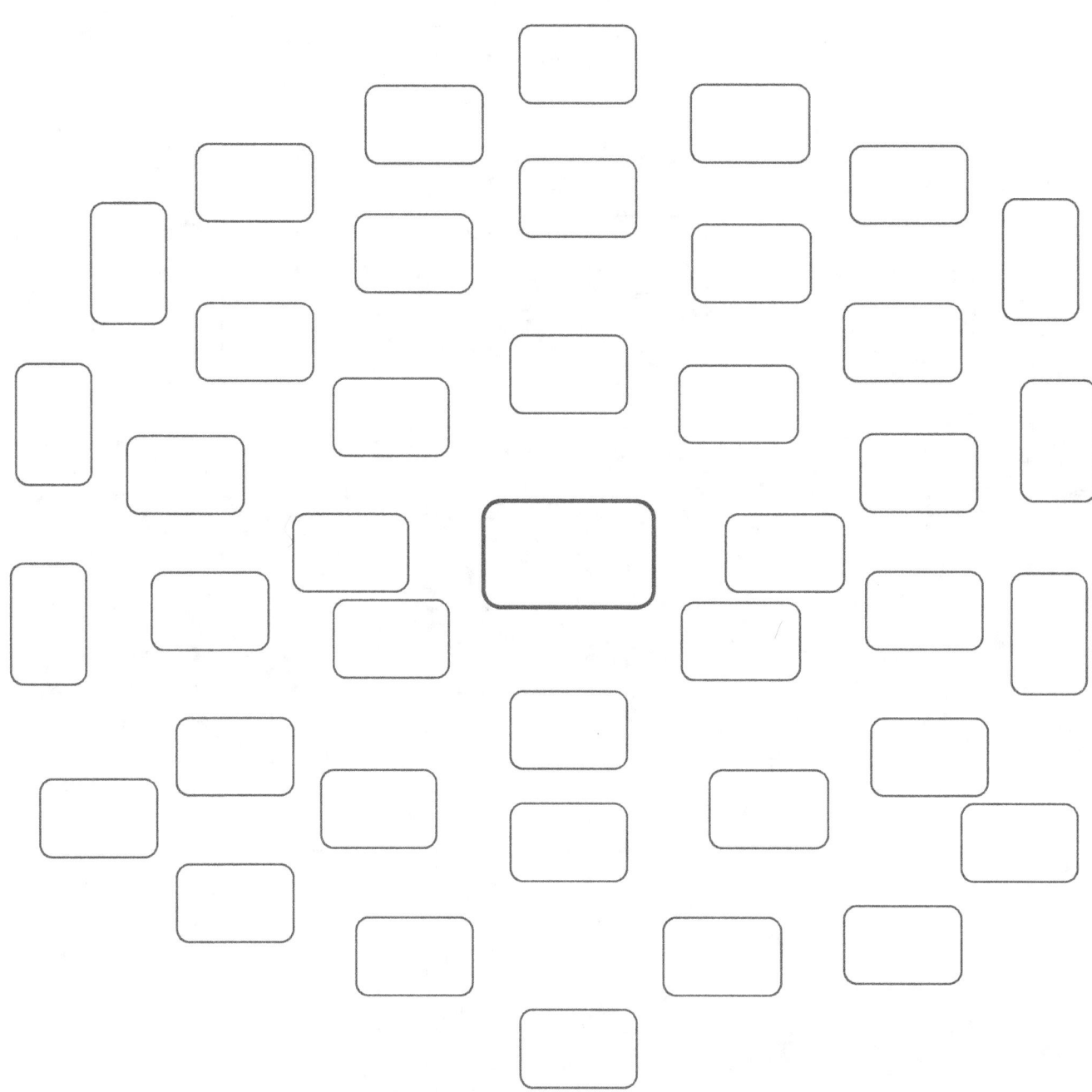

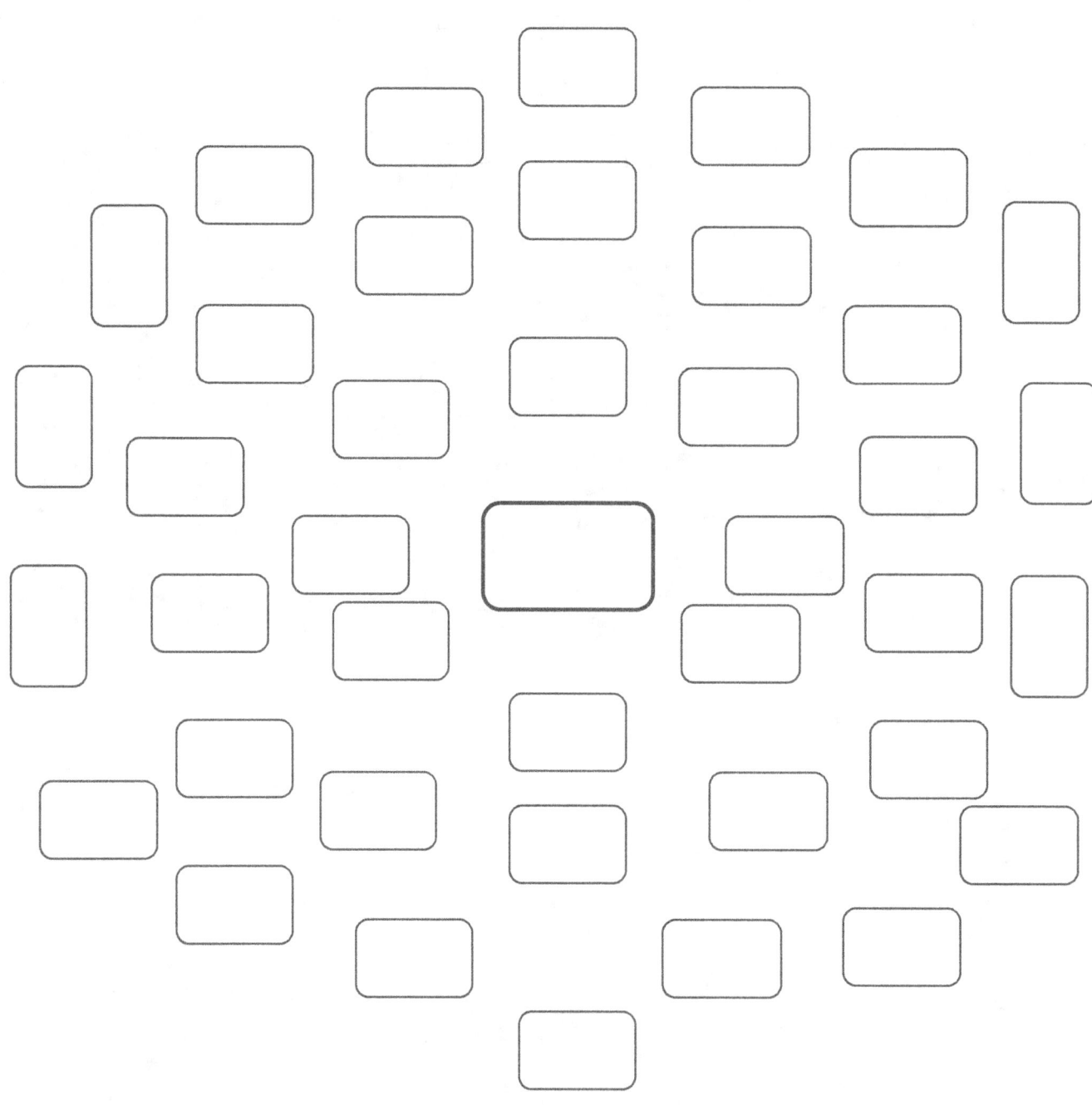

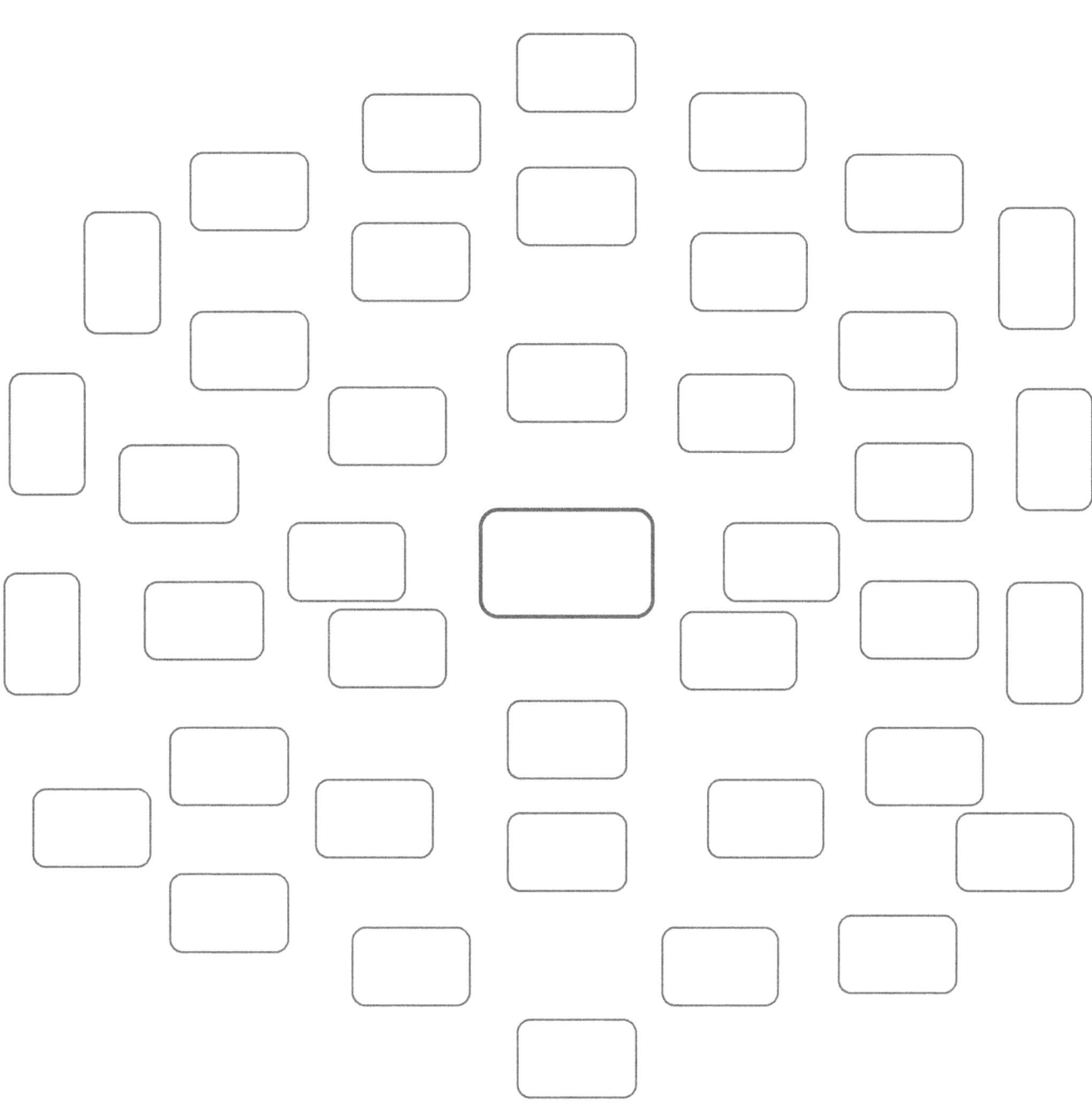

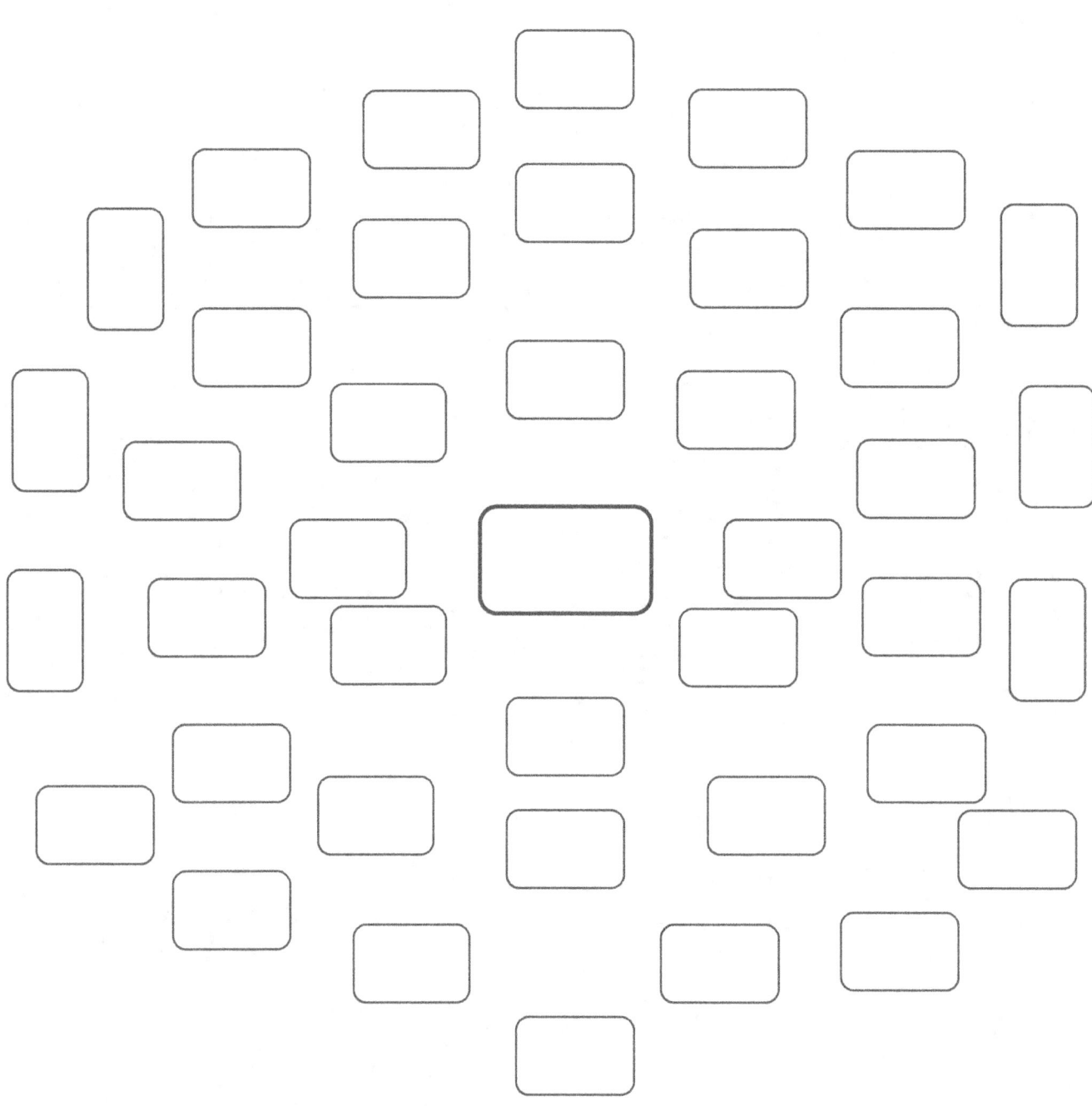

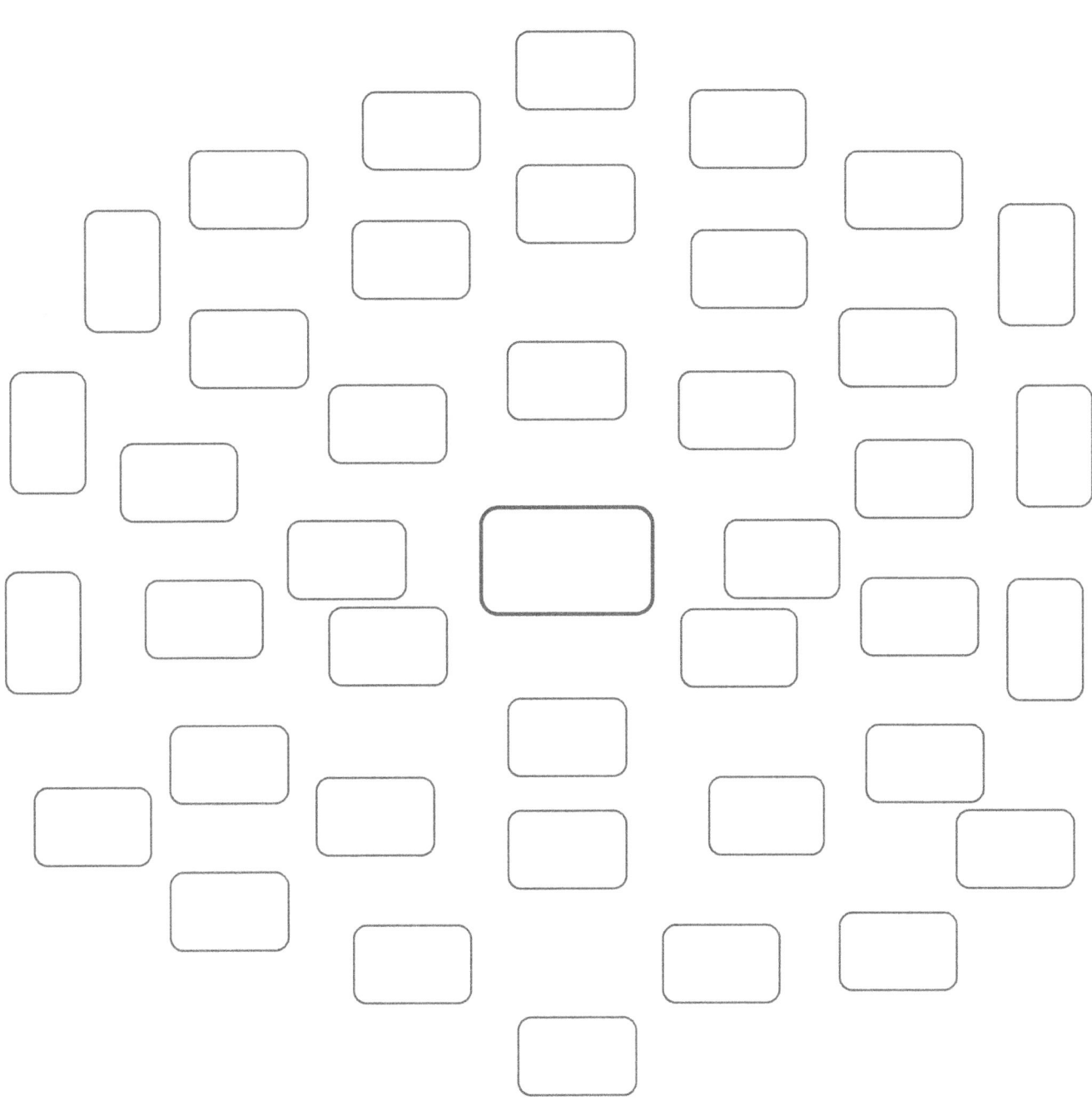

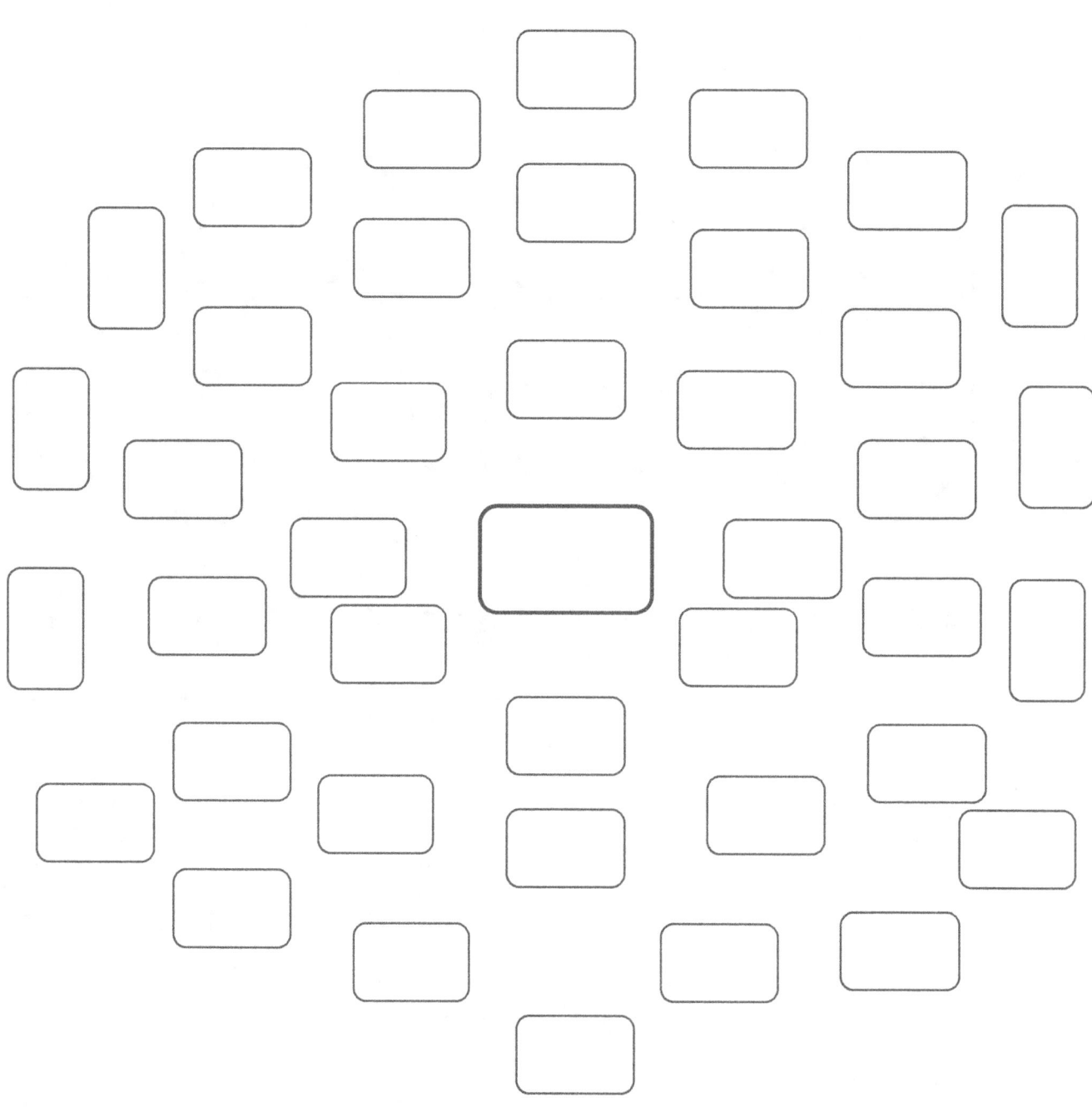

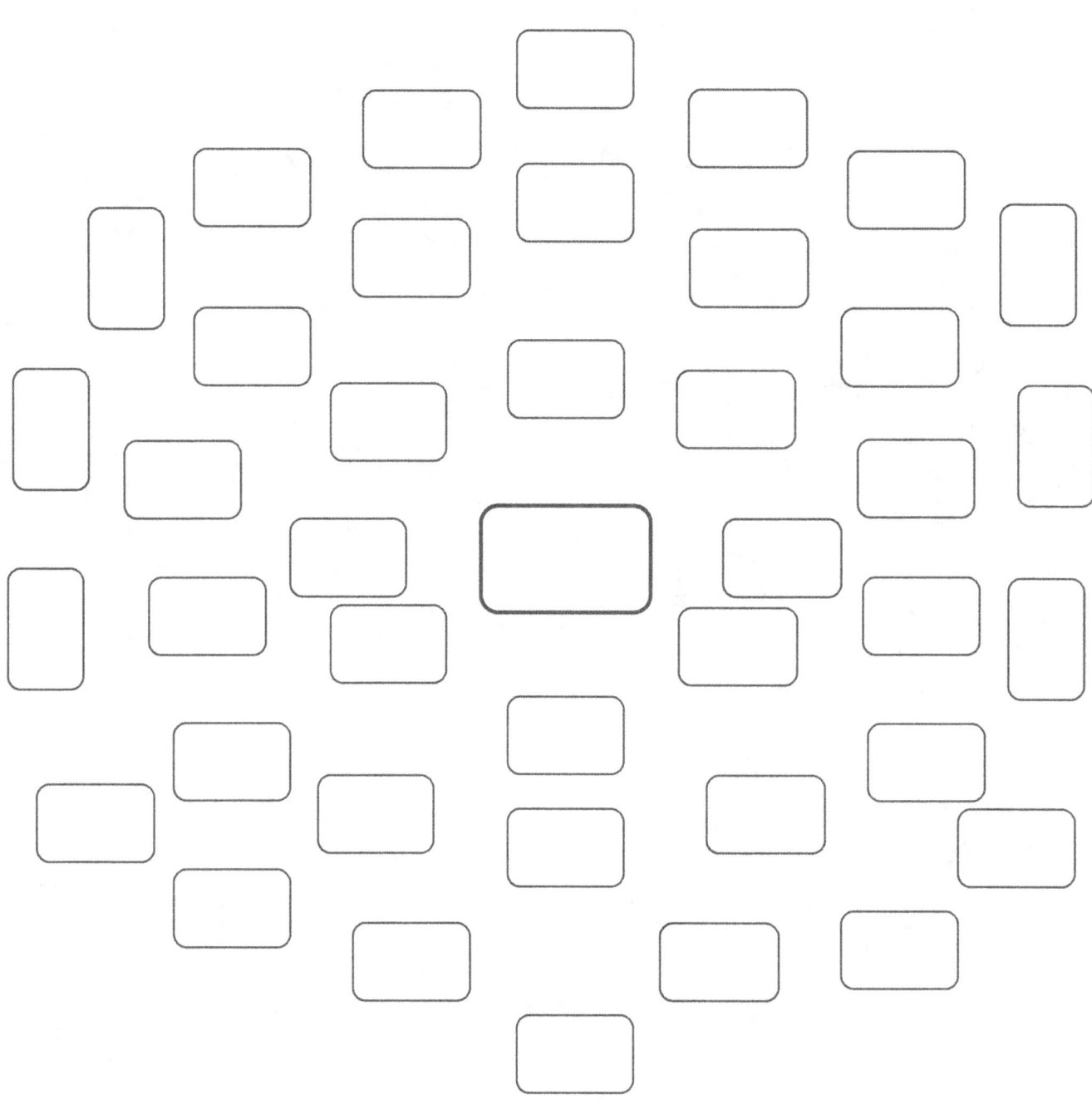

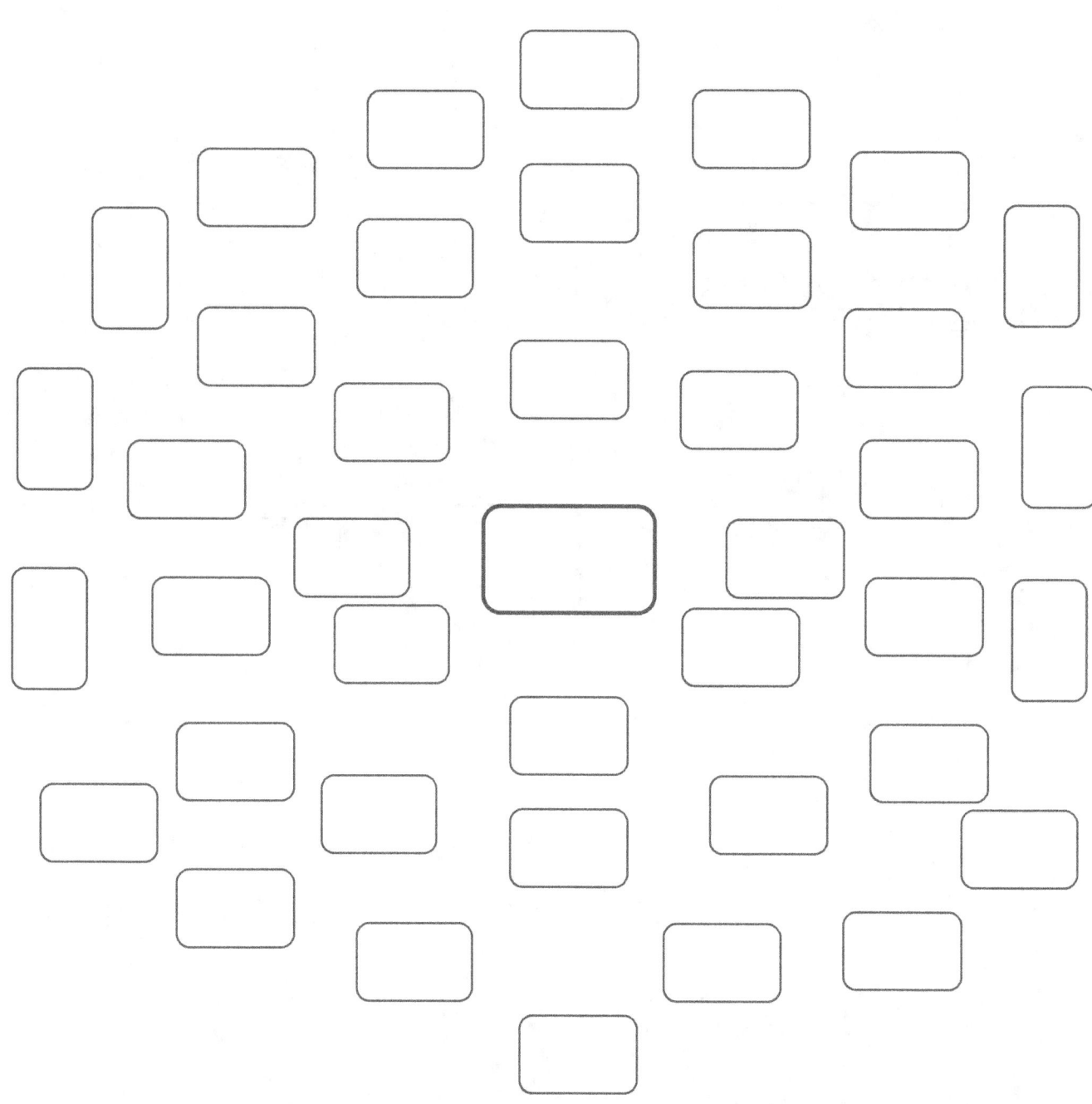

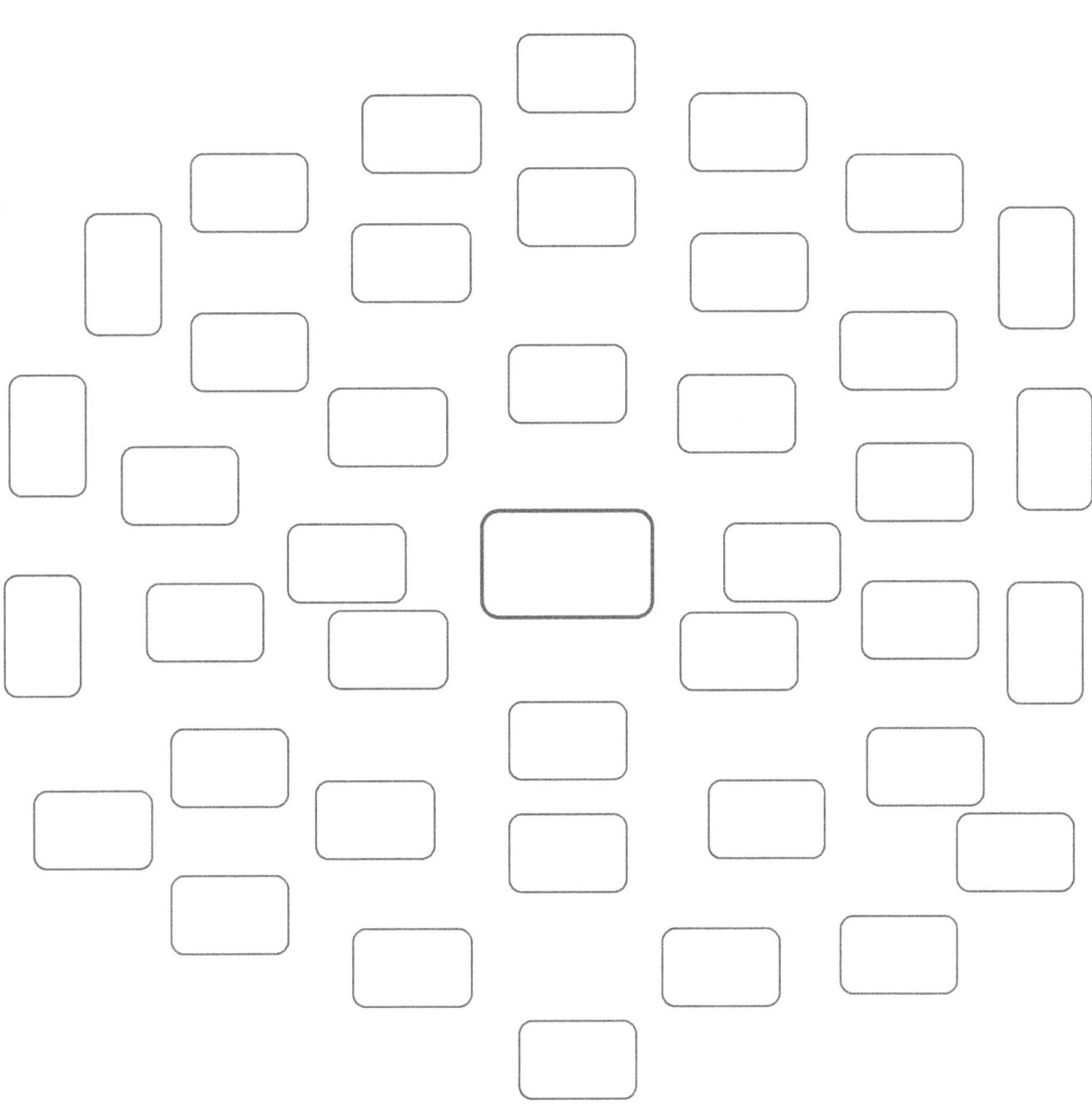

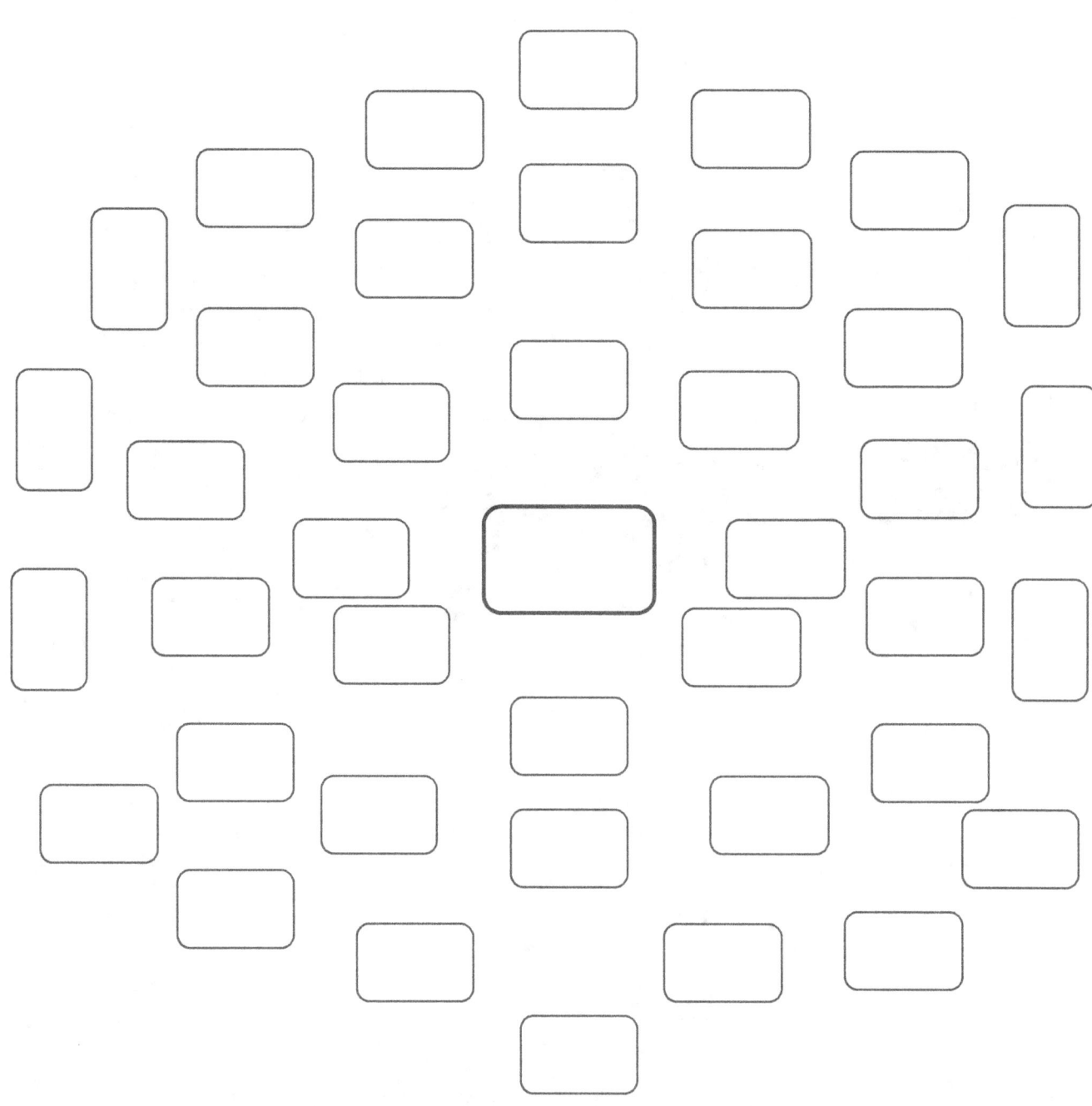

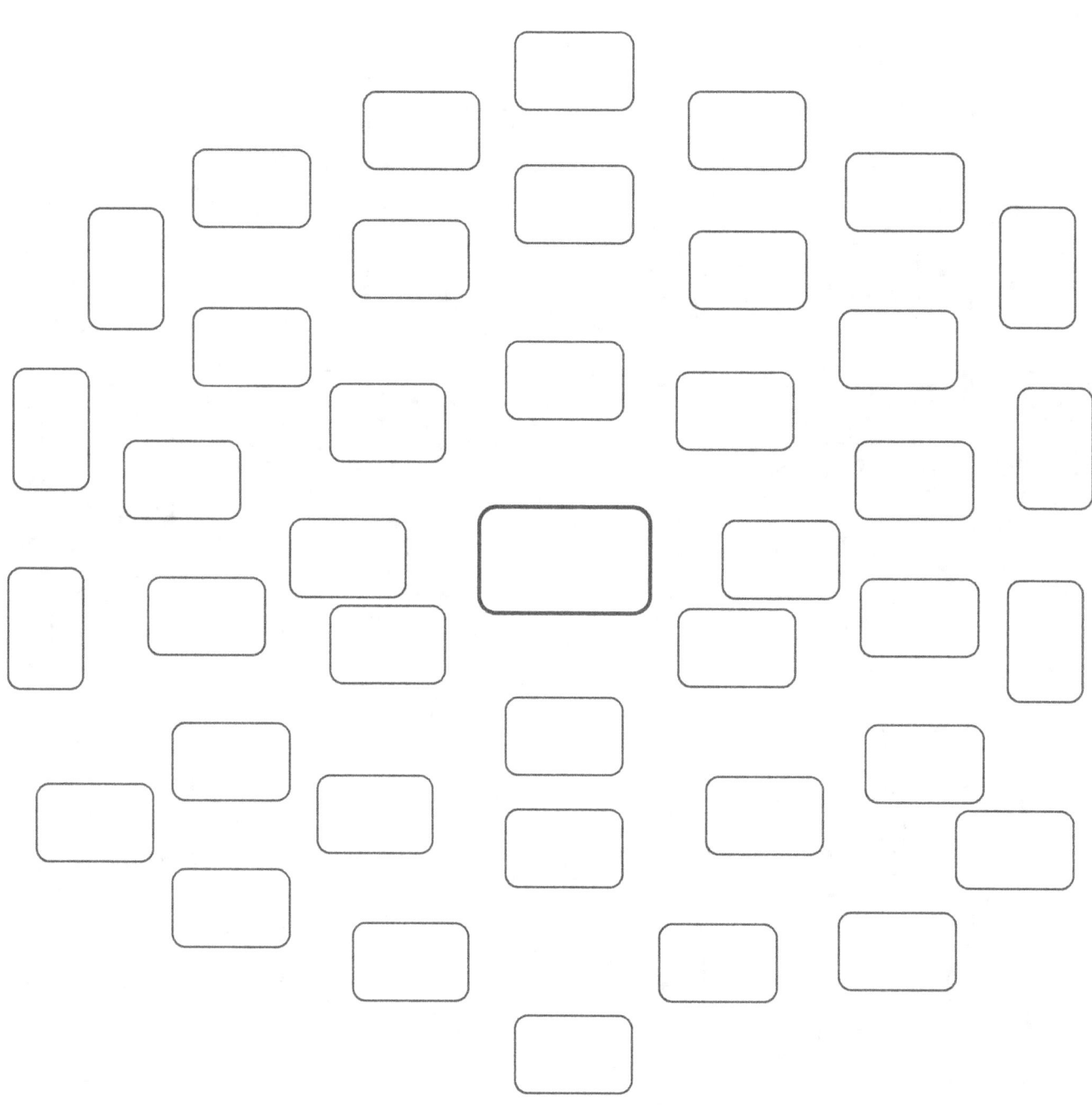

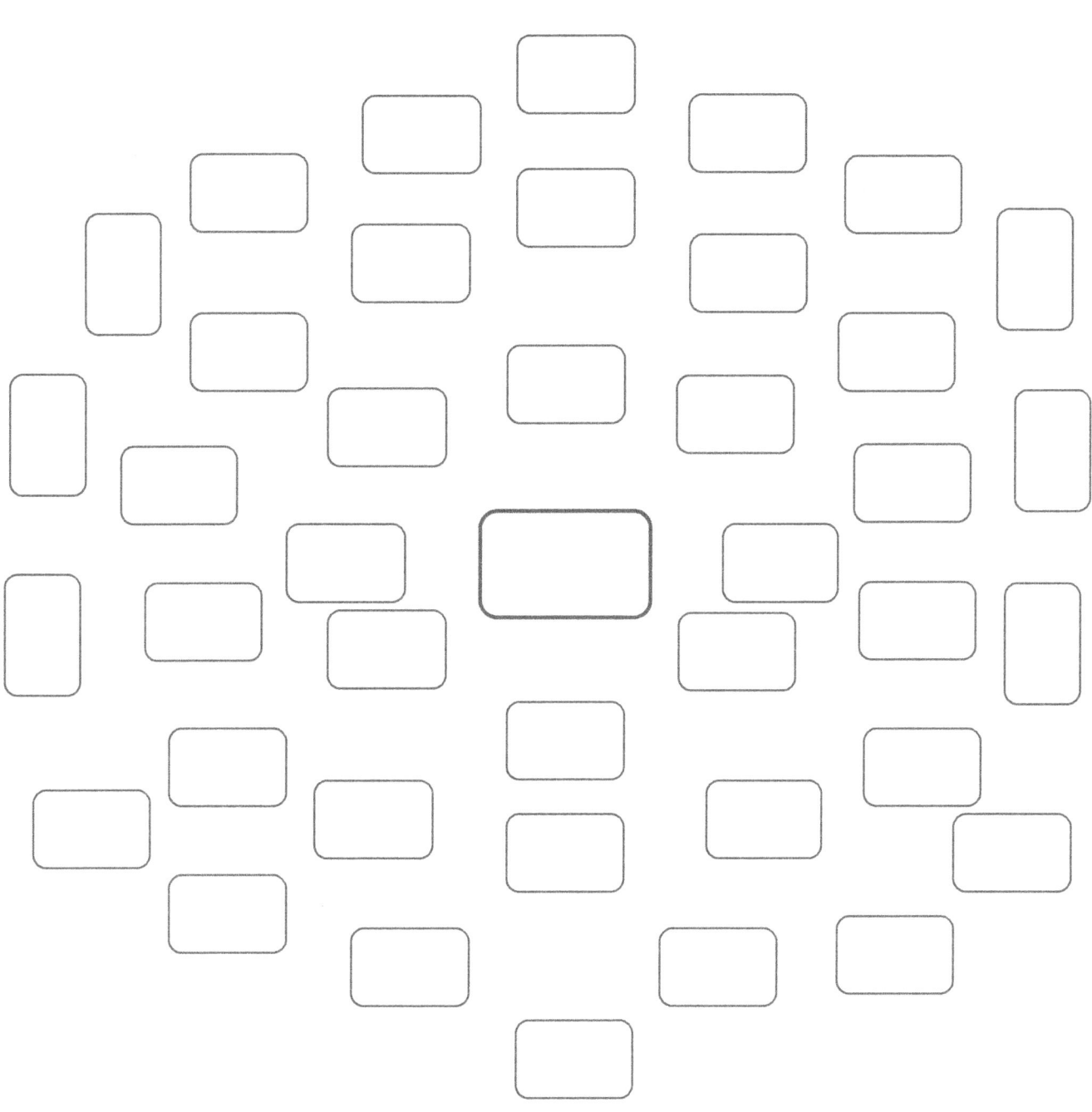

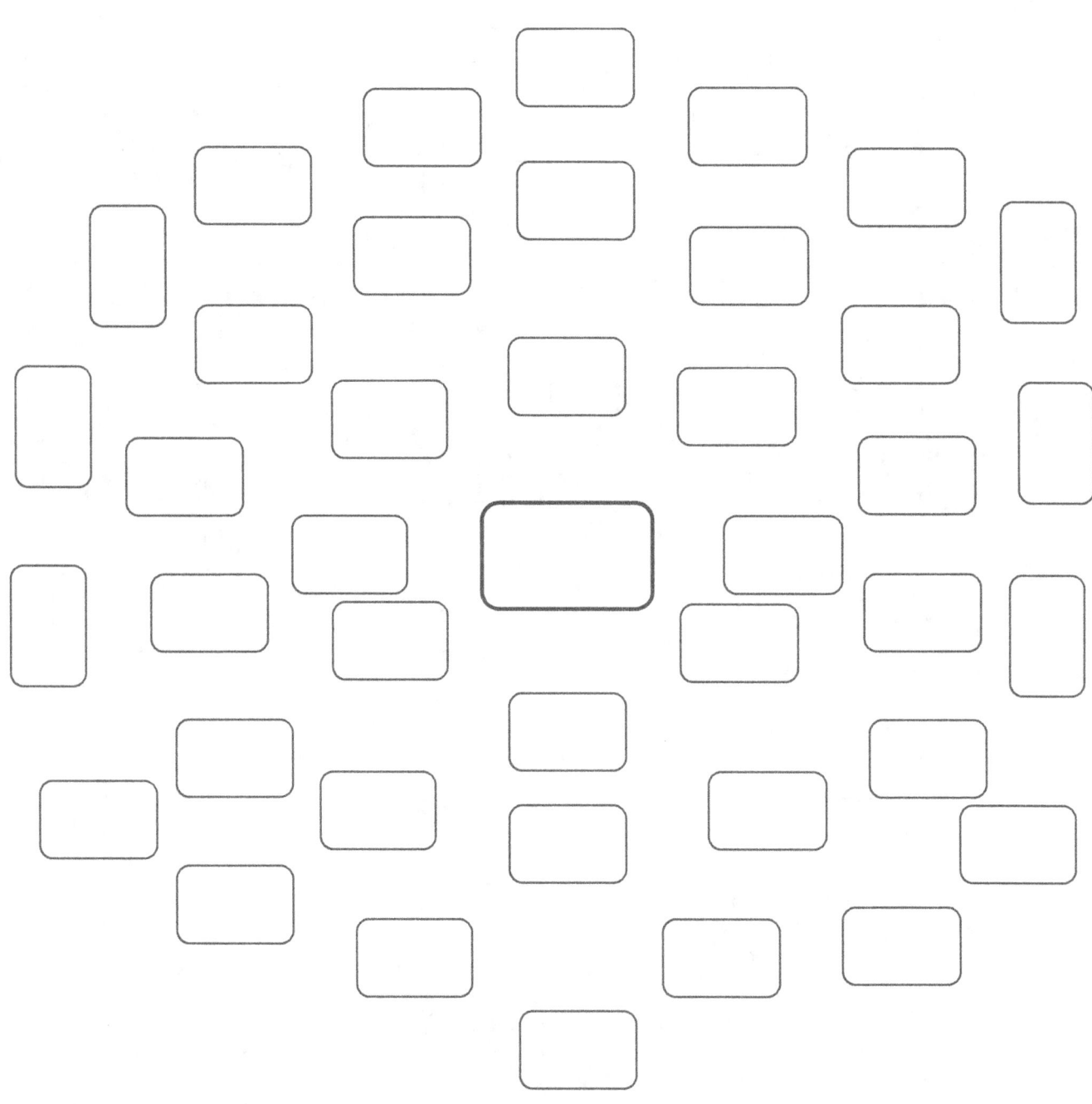

Good Job !

You have done it !

Cheer !

For more publish information, please scan the QR code.